I0009152

FORWARD

Thank you very much for purchasing "***The Strategy Session Volume 2 Getting Ready and Structure First***". I am Louis Ellman. I am one of the teachers of the AdvanceTo Training and Consulting Company. We teach MS Word Legal Style for top tier law firms. Our students routinely do very well on agency test and law firm tests. We take people from beginners and when they are done, they are at expert level.

Part of what we do is to teach a style that uses what we term Getting Ready and Structure First. This style enables one to save approximately 15-20 minutes off of a hands-on test. For everyday use, this routine prepares the screen in a way that places the maximum amount of information at your fingertips thus taking care of vital settings without you having to be concerned about those settings.

In this book, I am also going to share other tips of the trade that really make an absolute difference in your everyday work.

This is my second Teacher Connected Book so as in book one, reach out to me with any questions and/or any problems I can assist you with.

At the end of the book, for those of you that wish to experience our style of training from Basic through Advanced I will give you our offerings. If you wish to reach me or talk to us concerning our training as well as test creation or course creation, you can reach us at 1-888-422-0692 and my Extension is 2. My email is louis@advanceto.com.

I hope you enjoy this book "***The Strategy Session Volume 2 "Getting Ready and Structure First***".

Regards,

Louis

TABLE OF CONTENTS

CHAPTER 1. GETTING READY TO GET READY 1

CHAPTER 2. GETTING THE CCVER PAGE DONE 6

CHAPTER 3. STRUCTURE FIRST, THEN STYLE THE DOCUMENT 10

CHAPTER 4. SETTING THE PAGE NUMBERING FOR A SHORT TOC, TOA AND INDEX OF TERMS 12

CHAPTER 6. SUMMARY FOR SETTING THE PAGE NUMBERING FOR SHORT TOC'S, TOA'S AND INDEX OF TERMS 17

CHAPTER 7. SETTING UP THE PAGES FOR A LONGER TOC, TOA AND INDEX OF TERMS 17

CHAPTER 8. PUTTING IN YOUR PAGE NUMBERS FOR THE LONGER TOC, TOA AND INDEX 19

CHAPTER 9. SCHEDULES AND EXHIBITS THAT APPEAR UNDER THE TOC 22

CHAPTER 10. DEALING WITH THE PAGE NUMBERING FOR THE MAIN PART OF THE DOCUMENT 25

CHAPTER 11. DEALING WITH THE PAGE NUMBERING FOR THE EXHIBITS OF THE DOCUMENT 27

CHAPTER 12. INCLUDING EXHIBIT LETTERS IN YOUR TOC 29

CHAPTER 13. TRICKS OF THE TRADE 34

CHAPTER 14. MAKING USE OF THE CLIPBOARD WHEN APPLYING STYLES 37

CHAPTER 15. CHANGING THE FONT FOR THE ENTIRE DOCUMENT 39

CHAPTER 16. QUOTES SMART VS. STRAIGHT 40

CHAPTER 17. BONUS RUNNING A TABLE OF CONTENTS IN TWO COLUMNS 47

CHAPTER 18. CONCLUSION 53

CHAPTER 1.
GETTING READY TO GET READY

I feel that this is an important chapter. I go over this routine with all of my students. It helps get them set up in a way where they have access to a lot of information and the setup is one that provides consistency in how they go about their business from document to document.

So what is the routine we go through before we settle down to do a document?

1.　　Go to **File**, **Options** and under **Options** go to **Display**. There are three items under Display that I want to touch upon.

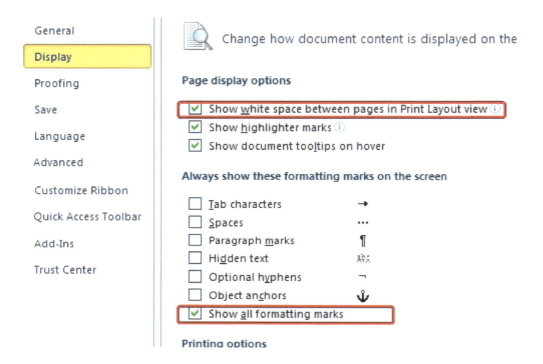

2.　　Above, we see **Show white space between pages in Print Layout View**. This ensures that when we are in **Print Layout View**, that you can see your Headers and Footers even though you are not inside the Header or Footer. If this is **not** turned on, you will not see your Headers and Footers in Print Layout View. You will simply see a green divider line where the page breaks.

3.　　Secondly, under **Display**, you have **Show all formatting marks**. This will ensure that when our **Show/Hide** button is turned on, ¶ that we can see our **tab characters**, **spaces**, **paragraph marks**, and any other formatting marks. Without this feature turned on it is like operating blind. You Show/Hide Button is under your Home Tab.

4.　　**Note**: One more **File**, **Options**, **Display** item to check on. That item is **"Print Drawings Created In Word"** (as shown in the picture below). This is important because if it is **unchecked**, then items that you created using text boxes, and auto shapes such as used in cascading paragraphs and Red Herrings, will not print and will not show up on the Print Preview. Now, if you do not know why it is not printing, you will waste a lot of time until you figure out. The attorney, the coordinator, the secretary, the IT guys will all be stressed so do remember to make sure it is checked. **Note**: I also checked in particular, "**Update Fields Before Printing**". This will make sure that **Page Numbering**, **TOC**, **TOA**, **Index of Terms Field Codes**, **Cross References**, etc., will all update before the document goes to print.

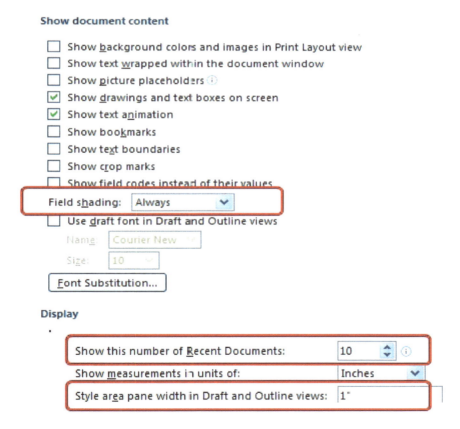

5. Under **File Options Advanced,** we will take care of another three items. They are "**Field Shading Always**", **Show Number of Recent Documents** and "**Style Area Pane**"

6.   **Field shading** as shown above, should be set for "**Always**" and that will ensure that things such as **Page Numbering**, **Table of Contents**, **Table of Authorities** and **Index of Terms** as well as **List Numberings**, **Cross References**, **Outline Numberings** etc. all have the grey shading to indicate that those items are automated items. For example your page numbering would look like this with field shading on 2.

7.   **Show This Number Of Recent Documents**. Set it to at least 10. In this way, if the attorney asks you to look for a document you did earlier, it should appear on your recent documents list. Some people set it to 25 but that may not be necessary. At least you know where the setting is that allows you to affect the number of recent documents.

8.   **Style area pane** refers to your **left side Style tracking panel** when you are in **Draft view** which is the old **Normal view**. In order to be able to see the left side tracking panel we always set the panel to **1 inch**. Just remember that in order to modify styles from the left side tracking panel just **double click** on any style in the left hand panel. **Right Click** on any style in the **right side Styles panel** in order to modify. *Double Click Left and Right Click Right to Modify styles is for you to remember*!

9.   Moving right along, under **Home,** go to **Style** on the right hand side and turn on your Style Area Pane by clicking on the little box to the right of the word "**Style**". That will open up your right side Style Panel.

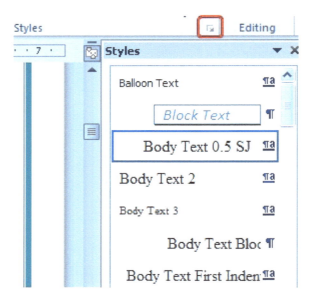

10.   At the bottom of your style area pane, click on **Options** and under **Select styles to show:** choose "**All Styles**" and "**Alphabetical**." Now you should see a full style palate.

11.   Go to **Page Layout** (**Layout** from 2016 on) and under **Page Setup** click on the little box 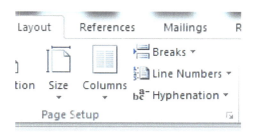 and we want to check on our Margins and our Section Break types.

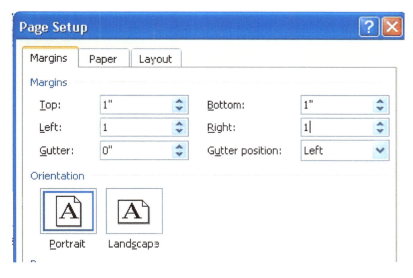

12   Our margins should be 1 inch Top, Bottom, Left and Right.

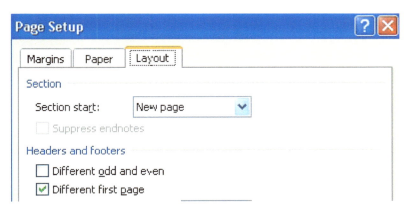

13.   Under **Layout**, Section Start should be "**New Page**" and under Headers and Footers, **Different First Page** as shown above applied to **Whole Document**.

14.   Almost done. Under your **View Tab**, make sure that your Ruler is **turned on** and switch over to "Draft View".

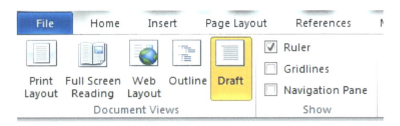

15.   Finally, on your **Status Bar** on the bottom of your screen, **right click** and make sure that your **Page Number**, **Section Number** and **Formatted Page Number** at the very least are all turned on. Just so you know, the **Page Number** is the **actual page** of the entire document that you are on at the moment. The **Formatted Page Number** reflects the number that it says as the number for that page based on **how you set up your page numbering**. So, while I may be on page 6 of the actual document, it may have a Page **3** at the bottom in the footer based on my page numbering setup. So, that is my **official routine** that I give to all of my students before we ever start our documents. Also, at the very bottom, make sure your Zoom and Zoom Slider is turned on so that you have the ability to affect the text size easily. **Zoom** and **Zoom Slider** will appear on the bottom right of your screen.

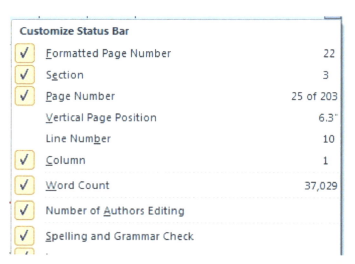

CHAPTER 2.
GETTING THE COVER PAGE DONE

This concept will serve you whether you are working in a law firm or you are taking a hands on test at an agency or law firm. If you put together the structure of the brand new raw text document first, then the styling of the document is a lot easier to do. What do I mean by structure? Let's go over the structure of the document.

1.   We start out with the **Cover Page** of the document. On the cover page of the document, you should make a **Section Break**, which should be a **Next Page** type of Section Break with the selection "**Different First Page" selected under Page Setup**. The **Vertical Alignment** of the cover page under **Page Setup, Layout**, will be "**Vertical Alignment Center**". The Vertical Alignment Center, should be applied to "This Section Only", while the remainder of the document is **ALWAYS** "**Top Alignment**". **Note**: Keep in mind that when a cover page is more involved and things are going on from top to bottom then **Vertical Alignment Center** may **not** be necessary. Short titles for sure, on cover pages should use **Vertical Alignment Center**.

2.   The text of the Cover Page should have a style associated with it called **Cover Page Text**. In this way, you do not leave the cover page text of the document in "**Normal**" style. It will result in points being taken away on a test if you leave the cover page text in Normal style and if at work, it is looked upon as lazy. Finally, there should not be any page numbering on the cover page. Below we see the cover page, and the **Page Setup** selections for the cover page. Remember, you get to **Page Set-Up Dialog Box** from the **Page Layout** (**Layout** Tab 2016 and Beyond) and look for **Page Setup** at the bottom of that section.

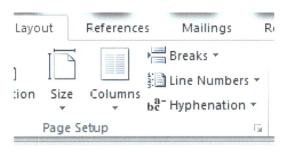

The **Cover Page Settings** are shown on the next page.

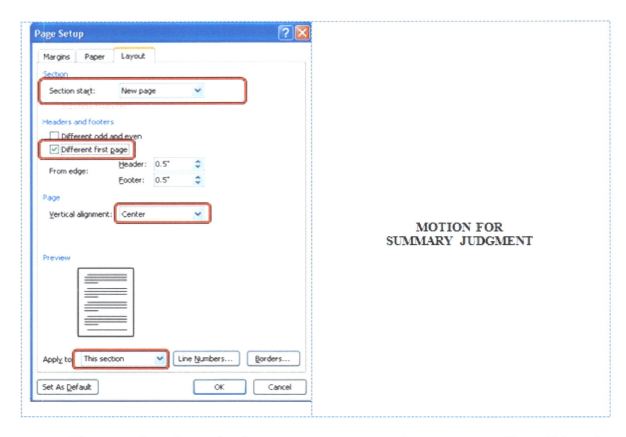

MOTION FOR
SUMMARY JUDGMENT

If you need to place a border on your cover page, then go to your Home Tab and

click on the "Page Border" button

Note: In the MS Word 2007-10 version you can find "**Page Border**" under the "**Page Layout**" Tab. In the **2013-16 version**, Page Border can now be found under the "**Design**" tab (right side). It is also worthy to note that the same is true for **Watermark** as well. Finally, you can get to the **Page Border** (contained in the **Border and Shading Dialog Box**) under the **Home Tab** by going to the **Borders Icon that sits next to** the "**Shading**" **Paint Can (as shown above in the** Red circle**)**. Once you click on the down arrow, go straight down to **Borders and Shading**.

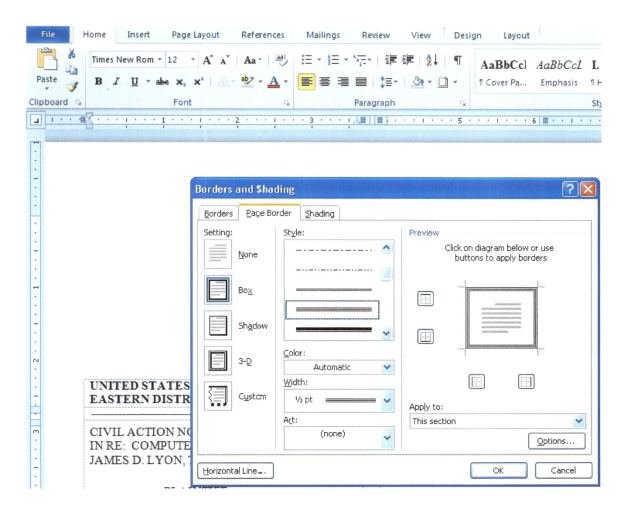

6.   As shown above, under the **Borders and Shading dialog box**, select **Page Border**, select your **border style** and apply to "**This Section**" as shown above. This is a common test question to see if you can apply the box to just one section and not have it on the entire document.

```
UNITED STATES DISTRICT COURT
EASTERN DISTRICT OF NEW YORK
                                                    x

CIVIL ACTION NO. 03-150-ABC
IN RE: COMPUTER CO., INC., DEBTOR
JAMES D. LYON, Trustee of Computer Co., Inc.        CASE NO. 02-12345

              PLAINTIFF                             ADV. NO. 03-12345

V.


BETTY GRAY, et al.

              DEFENDANTS
                                                    x

         REPLY MEMORANDUM OF LAW IN SUPPORT OF DEFENDANTS
            JOHN DOE AND JOE SMITH'S MOTION TO |
         DISMISS COUNTS FIVE AND NINE OF THE ADVERSARY COMPLAINT
```

7.   Your cover page is now vertically aligned center, and a **Page Border** has been applied. **Take note:** In this case, I **horizontally aligned** the cover page text as well. Sometimes, we will **NOT** vertically align the cover page with the caption when there is information at the bottom left of the cover page pertaining to the firm, the attorney involved and the address and phone. In that case **we balance out the page** to the best of our ability. The **most common** error when doing a cover page has to do with accidently applying **Vertical Alignment Center** to the "**Whole Document**" opposed to "**This Section**" only. You can always tell when this mistake has been made because when you have a short page within the document, the paragraph of that short page will be sitting in the **CENTER OF THE PAGE** rather than at the **TOP OF THE PAGE** as usual (**vertical alignment top**). When this mistake is made, there will not be any extra **before or after spacing** under "Paragraph" but if you look under **Insert Header** and you click on **Edit Header**, you will notice that the Header takes up **half your page** thus pushing down on whatever text is on the page in order to center it **vertically** and that is your tell-tale sign that **Vertical Alignment Center** is in use. Look at the sample Heading picture below.

Header

8.   It should also be noted that people who don't know to use **Vertical Alignment Center** under **Page Setup** try to vertically align the cover page text by either using **a bunch of hard returns to push down on the text** or, they use **a lot of Before and/or After Spacing** in order to attempt to visually vertically align the text. The only acceptable way is to use **Vertical Alignment Center**.

CHAPTER 3.
STRUCTURE FIRST, THEN STYLE THE DOCUMENT

1.   **The Table of Contents, Table of Authorities and Index of Terms page**. So, as part of the structure, now we want to take care of these above mentioned pages. By creating the pages and having them in place ready to go, after we format our document later on, all we need to do is to come back to our waiting pages and run the **TOC**, **TOA** and **Index of Terms**. That is a load off of your mind when the pages are sitting there waiting for you.

2.   **Note**. We will first deal with the set-up of a short Table of Contents, Table of Authorities, and Index of Terms. If you have a short TOC, TOA and Index, then after your **TOC Page**, make a **PAGE BREAK**, after your **TOA Page** make a **PAGE BREAK** and after your **Index of Terms page** make a **SECTION BREAK NEXT PAGE**. **Note:** You need the **Section Break Next Page** after the **Index of Terms** page, because that will separate your Table pages (TOC, TOA and Index), from the first page of your actual legal document.

Also, it should be noted that the **TOC, TOA and Index** are numbered using the **Romanette Style** of numbering which is **i,ii,iii,iv**, etc. while the numbering system of the actual document (*main part of the document*) will be **Arabic 1,2,3,** etc. and that is the **main reason** why the **Section Break Next Page** is needed after the Index of Terms. You **MUST** have a Section Break between two separate numbering types in order establish a different page number type. Let us look at the pages as described in this paragraph The picture below is using "Draft View".

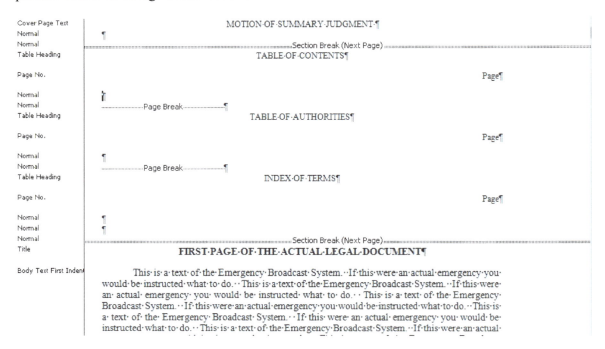

3.   So, if you look above, the Cover Page has a style called "**Cover Page Text**."

If you look at the Table of Contents page, assigned to the Table of Contents heading is sitting at the **top of the page** and **NOT** in the **header.** We gave it a style called "**Table Heading**" and the word "**Page**" which lies **right aligned** on the page (on the line below), we assigned it the style "**Page No**". as shown in the **left side panel** in the above picture. The "**Page No**" style simply Right Aligns the word "Page" and we build 12 Pts. After Spacing into the style in order to have space under the word Page.

Note: we used the **SAME STYLE** for the heading of the TOC, TOA and Index of Terms in order to **save valuable time.** There was **no need to make a style called** Table of Contents Heading, Table of Authorities Heading and Index of Terms Heading. The style "**Table Heading**" simply **centers the Heading** and puts in **12 points after** so it can be applied to all three headings without a problem. Whether you decide to make the Heading UPPERCASE, Title Case, **Bold** or <u>Underscore</u> is totally up to you but you will build that into your "**Table Heading**" style.

Note in the picture above, that we have an empty return on the left side of each page (TOC, TOA and Index) and it is in **Normal Style**. That empty return, **serves as the**

insertion point where you will place your cursor when you are ready to run the Table of Contents, Table of Authorities and Index of Terms **AFTER** you have styled your document. Below, we see a representation showing the **Cover Page** separated with a **Next Page Section Break** from the TOC, TOA and Index pages which are using the **Romanette style** page numbering.

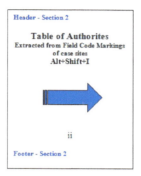

4.   Moving right along, some of you may ask what should I do with the structure, when I will have a **very long** TOC, TOA or Index of Terms? By very long, we are referring to a TOC, TOA and Index that exceeds one page. **Note**: If you are dealing with a large file, then you would set up your TOC, TOA and Index of Terms making use of your **Header** as we will see in **Chapter 5**:

CHAPTER 4.
SETTING THE PAGE NUMBERING
FOR A SHORT TOC, TOA AND INDEX OF TERMS

1.   We just went through setting up the document for a TOC, TOA and Index of Terms that has the **Headings on the top of the respective page** and not in the Header. We did that because we knew that they would not exceed one full page and it is a quick and easy set-up. Below, I will now show you how to set up your Romanette Page Numbering (**i,ii,iii**) for this type of set up that we discussed in **Chapter 3**. So here we go.

2.   As to the Page Numbering for the TOC. TOA and Index of Terms. Let us now set up the page numbering for these pages.

A.   Take your cursor over to the **empty return** on your **Table of Contents Page**.

B.   Go to **Insert** and Select **Footer**

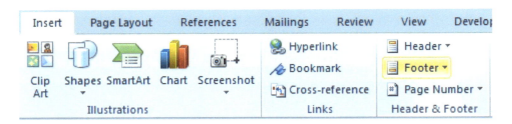

C.   Go down to **Edit Footer**.

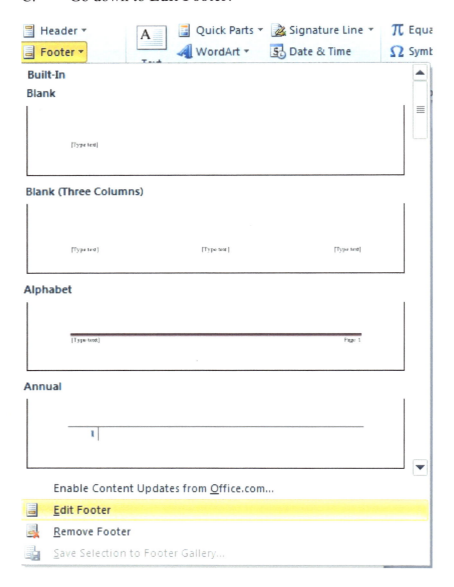

D.   Immediately turn off **Link to Previous**. Go to "**Page Number**" which is the **Third Button** from the **Left Hand Side** of the Header Footer Ribbon.

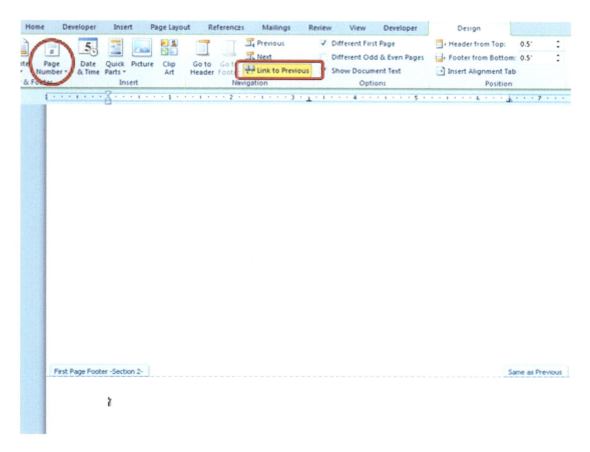

E.   Within the "**Format Page Number**" button, the only two items that you want to deal with are "**Format Page Numbers**" and "**Current Position**". Under **Format Page Number**, choose the **i,ii,iii** style of numbering and choose "**Start At "i"**". Press **OK** to exit the **Page Number Format Dialog Box**.

F.   Center your cursor. Use **Control + E** to do this.

¶

G.　　Go back to the "**Page Number**" button and go over to **Current Position** selection and choose **Plain Number**. Your "**i**" will now come in as expected.

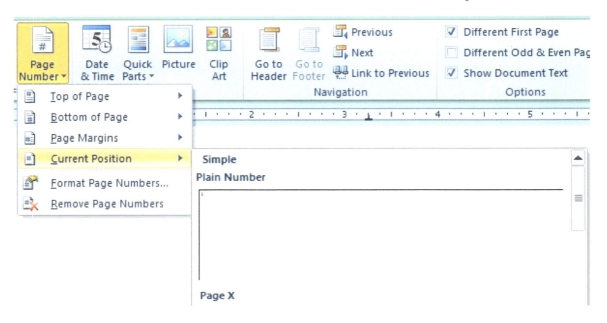

H.　　Your "**i**" will now be sitting in the center of the bottom of your page. **Note**: I had you use **Control E** to center the number rather than the "**Center Tab**" because using **Control E** will guarantee that the number always centers no matter what you do to the left and right margins. Conversely, the **Center Tab** in the ruler would have to be adjusted according to the **new** margin settings.

First Page Footer -Section 2-

I.   Go to the bottom of your **Table of Authorities** Footer. Take off **Link To Previous**.

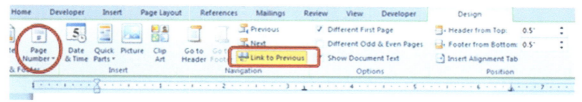

Take out any junk that may be in the Footer at this time. Make sure your cursor is **Centered** (Control + E) and go back to your **Page Number Button**, choose **Current Position** and **Plain Number**. The two little Romanette ii's should now appear.

J.   Go to the bottom of your **Index of Terms** Footer. Take off **Link To Previous**. Take out any junk that may be in the Footer at this time. Make sure your cursor is **Centered** (Control + E) and go back to your **Page Number Button**. The iii, should already be waiting at the bottom of your Index of Terms page. *This is so because once the second page of a particular section is set in terms of page numbering, you can be assured that the remainder of the section is good to go in terms of your page numbering.* That is why your Index of Terms was already good as to the Page Numbering since it was the third page of that section. You can now close your **Header and Footer Tool Bar** by clicking "**Close Header and Footer**" on the right side of your screen.

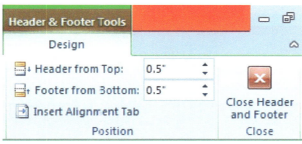

Footer -Section 2-

iii¶

CHAPTER 6.
SUMMARY FOR SETTING THE PAGE NUMBERING
FOR SHORT TOC'S, TOA'S AND INDEX OF TERMS.

1.   Select the Insert Tab

2.   Go to Footer,

3.   Edit Footer

4.   Turn off Link To Previous

5.   Go to your "Page Number" button. That is the **third button from the left** side of the Header/Footer Ribbon.

6.   Within your Page Number button, go to Format Page Numbers.

7.   Choose i,ii,iii and at the bottom Start at "i"

8   Center your cursor (**Control E**).

9.   Go back to your Page Number Button. Choose "**Current Position**", "**Plain Number**".

10.   Your number will now come in as intended.

11.   Repeat the process for the TOA and Index of Terms page using No. 9.

CHAPTER 7.
SETTING UP THE PAGES FOR A LONGER
TOC, TOA AND INDEX OF TERMS

1.   For this scenario, there will be a **Next Page Section Break between** the TOC and TOA. There will be a **Next Page Section Break between** the TOA and Index of Terms. There will be a **Next Page Section Break between** the Index and the first page of the actual legal document. Between each section of the TOC, TOA and Index of Terms, the **Romanette Style** Numbering (i,ii,iii), should *continue to run without restarting* from the TOC to the TOA to the Index etc. It is perfectly fine to **continue** the Romanette style number throughout the 3 sections.

2   **Important:** Table of Contents and the word Page would be placed in the "**First Page Header of the TOC Section**". **Table of Authorities and Page** would be placed in the "**First Page Header of the TOA Section** and finally, **Index of Terms and Page** would be placed in the "**First Page Header of the Index of Terms Section**.

3.   **Important To Note**: Until you run your TOC, TOA and Index, you will not have your second page of those pages so once you do run them you will then go back and establish the second page of each of those respective sections if needed. There is a

good chance that you will not have a spill over page for your TOA and Index but we will go over the entire process no matter what your scenario.

On the **SECOND PAGE** of the TOC heading for instance, it would say **Table of Contents** and directly underneath in parenthesis, it would say **(continued)**.

Look at the pictures below for the pattern and that same pattern would be repeated in your TOA and your Index of Terms Headers if in fact they spill over to an additional page. **Remember**: In order to be able to have a different Header for the page that spills over as the second page of your TOC for instance, you will have to make sure that under **Page Layout (Layout for 2016 and beyond)** and **Page Set-up** that the selection "**Different First Page**" is selected under **Layout**.

Remember!   Without Different First Page, you **can't** have the word "**(continued)**" on the second page of that Header and Table of Contents "**by itself**" on the **First page** of the Header.

Tip: When you set **Different First Page** under **Layout**, always set it for "**Whole Document**" and the ability to do something on one page of a section opposed to something different on the next page of that same section, will always be active! **TAKE NOTE:** On the First Page of each individual Header for instance, it will say First Page Header Section 2 (or whatever section you are on), and the second page of that **SAME SECTION** will say Header Section 2. The mention of "**First Page Header**" is your **CHIEF** indicator that **Different First Page is ACTIVE**.

TABLE·OF·CONTENTS¶

Page¶

First Page Header -Section 2-

TABLE·OF·CONTENTS¶
(continued)¶

Page¶

Header -Section 2-

Section Break (Next Page)

Table·of·Authorities¶

Page¶

First Page Header -Section 3-

Page Break

Table·of·Authorities↵
(continued)¶

Page¶

Header -Section 3-

·······Section Break (Next Page)·······

Index|of·Terms¶

Page¶

First Page Header -Section 4-   ·······Page Break·······

Index·of·Terms↵
(continued)¶

Page¶

Header -Section 4-

·······Section Break (Next Page)·······

4.   **Note**: It should be noted that when the Table Headings (TOC, TOA and Index) are set up using the **Header Page** as I show above, you **DO NOT NEED TO** use styles within the Header.

CHAPTER 8.
PUTTING IN YOUR PAGE NUMBERS
FOR THE LONGER TOC, TOA AND INDEX

The Table of Contents Page.

1.   Place your cursor on your Table of Contents Page.

2.   Go to Insert, Footer and choose Edit Footer.

3.   Immediately turn off **Link To Previous**.

4.   Go to your Page Number Button. That is the Third button from the left hand side of your Header/Footer Ribbon.

5.   Go to Format Page Numbers. Choose the **i,ii,iii** style of numbering and choose Start At **"i".**

6.   Center your cursor (**Control E**). Go back to your "**Page Number**" button and go to "**Current Position**" and choose "**Plain Number**". You should now have a **"i"** in your footer.

The Table of Authorities Page.

1.   Place your cursor on your Table of Authorities Page.

2.   Go to Insert, Footer and choose Edit Footer.

3.   Immediately turn off **Link To Previous**.

4.   Go to your Page Number Button. Third button from the left hand side of your Header/Footer Ribbon.

5.   Choose **Continue From Previous Section**.

6.   Center your cursor. Use Control E to center.

7.   Go back into your "Page Number" button. Choose Current Position and Plain Number.

8.   You should now see 'ii"

The Index of Terms Page.

1.   Place your cursor on your Index of Terms Page.

2.   Go to Insert, Footer and choose Edit Footer.

3.   Immediately turn off **Link To Previous**.

4.   Go to your Page Number Button. Third button from the left hand side of your Header/Footer Ribbon.

5. Choose **Continue From Previous Section**.

6. Center your cursor. Use Control E.

7. Go back into your "Page Number" button. Choose Current Position and Plain Number.

8. You should now see "iii"

9. Your page numbers for the longer TOC, TOA and Index of Terms making use of the Headers for the Heading information should now be done.

CHAPTER 9.
SCHEDULES AND EXHIBITS THAT APPEAR UNDER THE TOC

10.13	Assignability and Parties in Interest	45
10.14	Counterparts	46
10.15	Amendment and Modification	46
10.16	Confidentiality	46
10.17	No Strict Construction	48

Schedules

Schedule 1.1	Knowledge
Schedule 3	Disclosure Schedule
Schedule 3.7	Licenses and Permits
Schedule 3.8	Material Contracts
Schedule 3.13	Financial Statements of the Holding Company
Schedule 3.14	Environmental Matters
Schedule 3.15	Insurance
Schedule 3.16(b)	Tax Matters
Schedule 4.5	Financial Statements of IWNA
Schedule 6.7	Pro-Forma Owner's Policy
Schedule 10.12	Pre-Approved Transferees
Annex 1	Funding Date Capital Contribution Commitment
Annex 2	Form of Amended LLC Agreement pinions
Annex 3	Equity Base Case Model
Annex 4	Key Project Documents Not Yet Executed
Annex 5	Forms of Legal Opinions
Annex 5-A	Form of Legal Opinion of Counsel to the Class A Equity Investors

This is a good chapter because although this scenario does not always surface every day, you will want to have been exposed to this set-up. What you see above is a **Schedules List** that appears under the completed **Table of Contents**. The Schedules list (which I will go over with you in a moment), sits underneath the active TOC as "**Static Text**". It is not meant to change or update so it is simply plain text. I would suggest with the set-up that you see above, that you use a **two column table**. Let us go over together, how to turn the text above into a two column table.

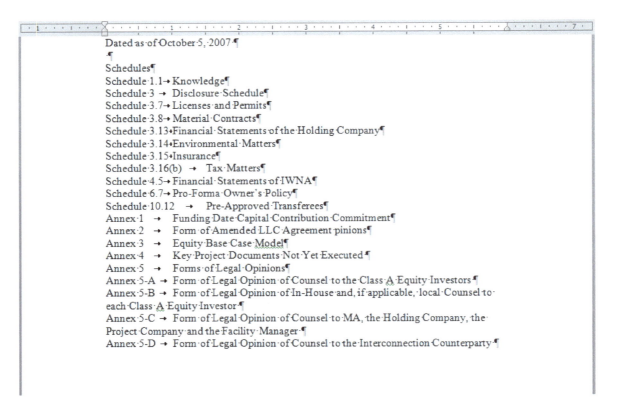

1.   In the MS Word Document, as shown above, I have placed a **TAB** between **each separate entry** of the Schedule or Annex Number and the title of the Schedule or Annex.

2.   Highlight the entire **Schedules** and **Annex Area**.

3.   Go to **Insert**, **Table** and choose **Convert Text to Table**.

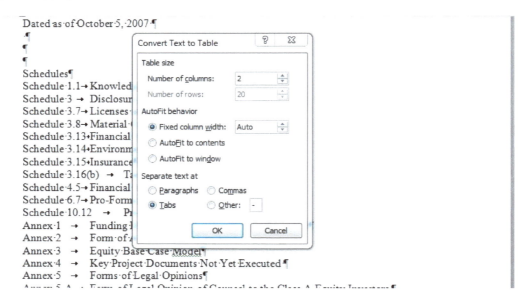

4.   "Number **of Columns" is 2** and under "**Separate Text At**" the selection "**Tabs**" will easily separate the text into two columns.

5.   To get rid of the Border Lines of the Two Column Table, select the entire table. **Tip**: If you are in "**Print Layout**" you can click on the "**Target Symbol**" on the left of the Table to quickly select the entire table.

6.

Schedules¤	¤	¤
Schedule·1.1¤	Knowledge¤	¤
Schedule·3¤	Disclosure·Schedule¤	¤
Schedule·3.7¤	Licenses·and·Permits¤	¤
Schedule·3.8¤	Material·Contracts¤	¤
Schedule·3.13¤	Financial·Statements·of·the·Holding·Company¤	¤
Schedule·3.14¤	Environmental·Matters¤	¤
Schedule·3.15¤	Insurance¤	¤
Schedule·3.16(b)¤	Tax·Matters¤	¤
Schedule·4.5¤	Financial·Statements·of·IWNA¤	¤
Schedule·6.7¤	Pro-Forma·Owner's·Policy¤	¤
Schedule·10.12¤	Pre-Approved·Transferees¤	¤

7.   With the Table Highlighted, go to your **Table Tools Menu** and under the **Design Tab**, select "**No Border**". Re-adjust the Table Column widths as necessary.

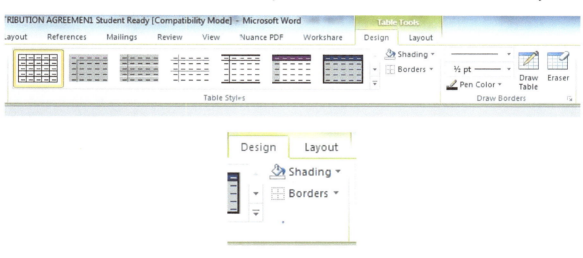

9.   Your Schedules list should now look like the one below.

Schedules¤	¤	¤
Schedule·1.1¤	Knowledge¤	¤
Schedule·3¤	Disclosure·Schedule¤	¤
Schedule·3.7¤	Licenses·and·Permits¤	¤
Schedule·3.8¤	Material·Contracts¤	¤
Schedule·3.13¤	Financial·Statements·of·the·Holding·Company¤	¤
Schedule·3.14¤	Environmental·Matters¤	¤
Schedule·3.15¤	Insurance¤	¤
Schedule·3.16(b)¤	Tax·Matters¤	¤
Schedule·4.5¤	Financial·Statements·of·IWNA¤	¤
Schedule·6.7¤	Pro-Forma·Owner's·Policy¤	¤
Schedule·10.12¤	Pre-Approved·Transferees¤	¤
Annex·1¤	Funding·Date·Capital·Contribution·Commitment¤	¤
Annex·2¤	Form·of·Amended·LLC·Agreement·pinions¤	¤
Annex·3¤	Equity·Base·Case·Model¤	¤
Annex·4¤	Key·Project·Documents·Not·Yet·Executed¤	¤
Annex·5¤	Forms·of·Legal·Opinions¤	¤
Annex·5-A¤	Form·of·Legal·Opinion·of·Counsel·to·the·Class·A·Equity·Investors·¤	¤
Annex·5-B¤	Form·of·Legal·Opinion·of·In-House·and,·if·	¤

CHAPTER 10.
DEALING WITH THE PAGE NUMBERING
FOR THE MAIN PART OF THE DOCUMENT.

1.   **Almost done**. Now you would set your Arabic page numbering (1,2,3) on the first page of the main part of the legal document. **Important:** You set the page numbering on **the first page** of the actual legal document but you *don't bring the numbering in* until the **second page footer** of that section.

2.   Place your cursor on the **first page** of the Section that represents the main part of the legal document.

3.   Go to Insert, Footer, **Edit** Footer.

4.   Immediately turn off **Link To Previous**.

5.   Go to your "**Page Number**" button. This is your third button from the left side of your Header Footer Toolbar.

6.   Go to Format Page Numbers. Choose 1,2,3 as the page numbering Style.

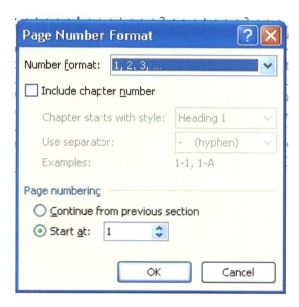

7. Choose OK. We **DO NOT** bring in the page number on page 1.

8. Go to the bottom of the **SECOND PAGE** of the main part of the document. This is the second page of that section. Immediately take off Link To Previous.

9. Take out any junk that may be in this footer.

10. Center the cursor. (**Use Control E**).

11. Go back into the "**Page Number Button**" (Third Button from the left hand side of the Header Footer tool bar).

12. Choose "**Current Position**" and "**Plain Number**".

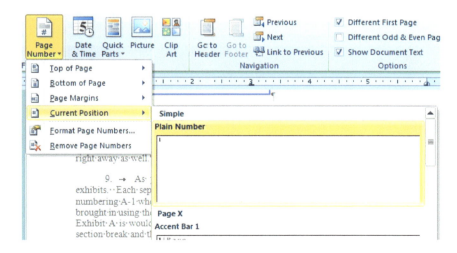

13. You should now see your Page "2" come in.

14. Your numbering will now be complete for the remainder of this section no matter how many page numbers there are in the main part of the document. It is **important to note** that the main part of your legal document is the only piece of the document, that **we do not start the page numbering on page one**. Your TOC, TOA and Index of Terms numbering starts the Page Numbering on Page 1 and your Exhibits start numbering right away as well.

15. **NOTE**: If the attorney wants dashes (also known as "**wings**") to be placed on either side of the page number in the main part of the document place them in manually, meaning type them in on either side of the Field Code. It will look like this -2-. Do not use the pre-sets that appear under "**Current Position**". If you should use a **pre-set**, then when you run your **Table of Contents**, the **Dashes** will be pulled into your **Table of Contents because they are part of the Field Code**. If you manually type in the **Dashes**, then they will not transfer into the **Table of Contents** and that is what you want.

CHAPTER 11.
DEALING WITH THE PAGE NUMBERING
FOR THE EXHIBITS OF THE DOCUMENT.

1. As part of the structure, examine your document to see if there are exhibits. **Each separate Exhibit, Annex or Schedule will need its own section**. So, for example, **Exhibit A** will have the page numbering A-1 where the A and the hyphen, are typed in **manually**, while the 1 of A-1 is brought in using the page number feature under Headers and Footers. So in the footer of Exhibit A, it would look like A-1. Between Exhibit A and Exhibit B there should be a **Section Break** and the page numbering for Exhibit B will look like this: B-1, B-2 and so on.

APPENDIX A¶
[LETTERHEAD OF AJAX NATIONAL INSURANCE COMPANY]¶
_____ __, 20__¶

Re: Maximum Annual Premium Volume¶

Dear:¶

      As required pursuant to that certain General Agency Agreement between AJAX NATIONAL Insurance Company ("AJAX"), and BOZO OF NEVADA, INC., (" BOZO"), please be advised that the maximum annual premium volume which BOZO is authorized to write on behalf of AJAX in each calendar year shall not exceed $____ → ____ → ____ → ____ .. Notwithstanding the foregoing, such maximum annual premium volume may be increased or decreased by AJAX at any time upon five (5) days written notice to BOZO.¶

          Very truly yours,¶

          AJAX National Insurance Company¶

          By: _____ → _____ ¶

LS:xx¶
cc: ¶ ....Section Break (Next Page)...

First Page Footer -Section 4-

A-1¶

2.   What if I have Schedules? Let us talk about Schedule 1. If you have a Schedule in the back, you can have for example, number S-1-1. If the actual name of the Schedule is Schedule 1 then that is the reason why I have placed S-1-1. Schedule 2 on the other hand could be numbered S-2-1 and so on. Note that wherever you see grey that is the auto number and wherever you see regular text that is the portion that **YOU** type in on the Footer.

3.   **So to sum up this section**. Structure first means **segment** the document into sections as needed. 1) Set the page numbering for the TOC, TOA, Index of Terms section. 2) Set the page numbering for the main part of the legal document and then turn your attention to 3) setting the page numbering for your Exhibits, Annexes of Schedules.

Once you have taken care of your structure, then go ahead and style the document from beginning to end. It will be a lot easier for you operating in this fashion. After you have styled the document, then all you need to do is to go back to your TOC page and run the Table of Contents, go to your TOA page and run the Table of Authorities and go to your Index of Terms and run that as well. This method once understood, will be very quick to set up and will give you more command of your documents. **Structure First!**

CHAPTER 12.
INCLUDING EXHIBIT LETTERS IN YOUR TOC

Most of the Time, we manually place Exhibit Letter into the Footer using Plain Text before the number Field Code that controls the number as we did in the last Chapter. Such as A-1. But once in a while, they want the A-1 in the actual TOC so I will show you how to set it up. Let us assume that we have a four level Multilevel Outline so that the first available Heading is Heading 5.

1.	Attach Heading 5 to the Heading of your first Exhibit as you see below.

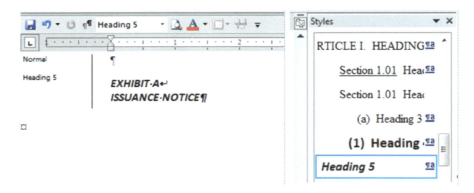

2.	Go to your Multilevel Dialog Box and Proceed to set it up in the following way for Heading 5. Remember to also **Link Level 5** to **Heading 5** so that the connection is made to the Heading style. I included the Font photo directly underneath this photo.

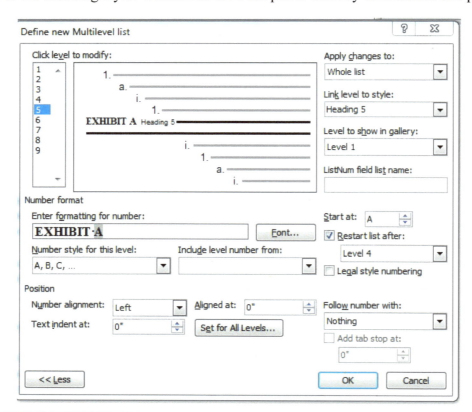

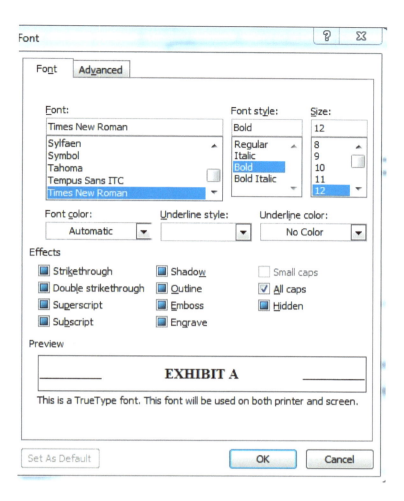

3.   Once you come out of the Multilevel Dialog Box go over to your right side panel and right click on the Heading 5 style and proceed to take care of Font and Paragraph settings for the Exhibit A Heading. The Textual Aspect of the Exhibit A Heading are the words "**ISSUANCE NOTICE**." The Number Aspect of Exhibit A is **EXHIBIT A**.

The **Font** of the **Textual Aspect** should look like the picture below.

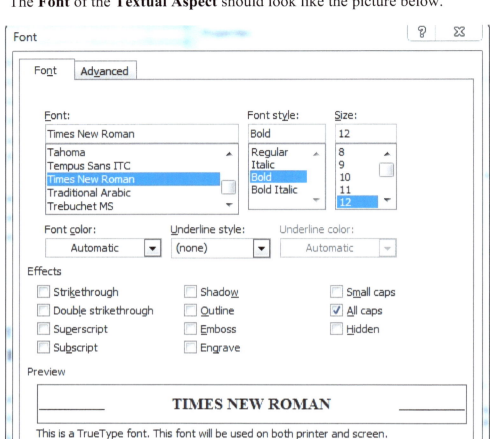

The Paragraph Settings For **Heading 5** should look like the picture below:

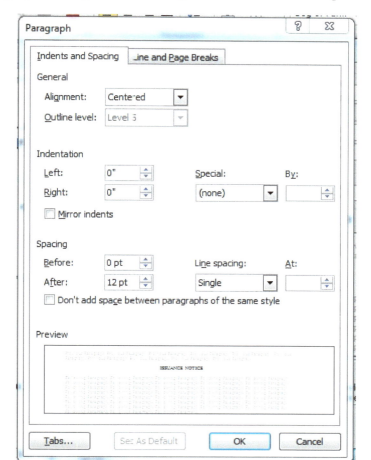

4.   Your **Exhibit A** Heading should now be in place/

EXHIBIT A↵
ISSUANCE·NOTICE¶

5.   Go to the Footer of Exhibit A. Insert Footer, Edit Footer, Turn Off "Link To Previous", Go to the "Page Number Button" which is the 3rd button from the left on your Header/Footer Ribbon.

6.   Once inside, go to **Format Page Number** and put in the following settings. **Note**: You are using "**Include Chapter Number**".

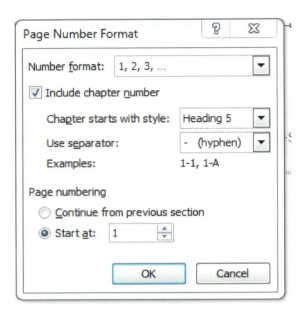

7.   Press OK and Center your cursor (Control E).

8.   Go back into your Page Number Button, look for "**Current Position**" and choose **Plain**.

9.   Your Footer will now have **A-** as part of the Field Code as shown below.

10.   Now, when you run the TOC remember to use Headings 1,2 and 5 which will generate the first two levels of your Multilevel Outline and your Exhibit(s) pages as shown below.

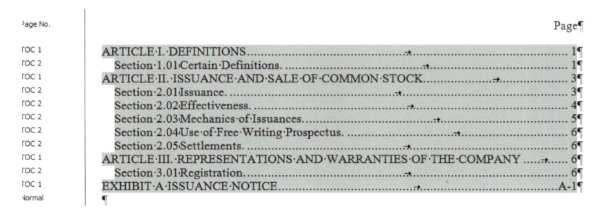

Page No.		Page¶
TOC 1	ARTICLE·I.·DEFINITIONS..→	1¶
TOC 2	Section·1.01·Certain·Definitions. ....→	1¶
TOC 1	ARTICLE·II.·ISSUANCE·AND·SALE·OF·COMMON·STOCK.................→	3¶
TOC 2	Section·2.01·Issuance. ....→	3¶
TOC 2	Section·2.02·Effectiveness. ....→	4¶
TOC 2	Section·2.03·Mechanics·of·Issuances..........................→	5¶
TOC 2	Section·2.04·Use·of·Free·Writing·Prospectus. ....→	6¶
TOC 2	Section·2.05·Settlements. ....→	6¶
TOC 1	ARTICLE·III.·REPRESENTATIONS·AND·WARRANTIES·OF·THE·COMPANY .....→	6¶
TOC 2	Section·3.01·Registration....................................→	6¶
TOC 1	EXHIBIT·A·ISSUANCE·NOTICE....................................→	A-1¶
Normal	¶	

CHAPTER 13.
TRICKS OF THE TRADE

Sample of numbers using Hard Space protection:

> Scheme·opponents·proffered·six·objections,·which·included·(1)°the·lack·of·jurisdiction·of· the· Court· to· sanction· the· Scheme· on· the· grounds· that· Luxury· Bank· failed· properly· to· constitute·creditor·classes;·(2)°claims·of·opposing·creditors·were·improperly·adjusted·for· voting·purposes;·(3)°those·who·votes·in·favor·had·special·interest·snot·representing·those· of· opponents;· (4)°the· Scheme· is· unfair· because· it· would· benefit· the· Company,· which· is· solvent,· by· allowing· a· release· of· surplus· to· its· shareholders· to· the· disadvantage· of· creditors;·(5)°that·insurance·and·reinsurance·creditors·interests·differed·from·those·with· Very· Untrue· Claims,· whose· contracts· would· be· effectively· rewritten· by· a· forced· commutation· of· their· liabilities,· since· it·would·be·impossible·to·value·fairly·such·claims;· (6)°Scheme· Creditors· would· be· unfairly· deprived· of· their·rights·of·access·to·the·courts;· and· that· (7)°certain· Scheme· provisions,· such· as· the· Company's· exclusive· right· to· terminate·the·Scheme·and·others·are·one·sided.··Id.·at·¶¶·45·53.¶

Let us start out by talking about the use of Hard Space and my little trick to take care of them as needed. **Hard Space** is also known as **Required Space** and **Non-Breaking Space**. If you look at the picture above, the numbers (1)-(7) within the paragraph are using hard spaces (the little Degree looking symbol) to make sure that numbers (1)-(7) do not separate from the word that "**directly**" follows the closed parenthesis.

A Non-breaking Space simply serves to keep two items together such as John Q Smith. A hard space would be placed between the John and Q so that the Q does not separate from John and wrap around to the next line leaving the name John at the end of the line by itself. Another example is January 1, 2017. We would place the Hard Space between the January and the 1 so that January 1 does not separate but acts like one piece of text.

Inserting Hard Spaces as Needed.

In order to make the Hard Space first make sure that there are no regular spaces between the two items that you wish to have stay as one piece.

1.   Place the cursor between the two items and do **Control + Shift** and tap the Space Bar **1X**.

2.   There should be only the hard space between the two items. If there is a **Hard Space** and a **regular space** it will not work.! When you insert a Hard Space, it produces a degree like symbol °.

What if there are many Instances of Items Needing Hard Space and time is of the Essence?

Many times while working on a document in the center, you see paragraph after paragraph that needs Hard Space protection. Well if you are in a position where an attorney is pressing the Coordinator to get the job back, you obviously are not going to be picking through a document looking for hard spaces to insert.

There are two things you can do in this situation.

1. After you have done all of your edits, look through the document keeping your focus on the right side of the page. You are looking for stragglers that are by themselves at the end of a line that are in need of a Hard Space.

2. You can also do a **global replace** if you so desire in order to take care of all hard space situations at one time. The most common use of the Hard Space is using it for situations whereby you have numbering systems within the paragraph such as the example I provided at the beginning of this Chapter. **Important**: Before I protect a paragraph for Hard Spaces using Find and Replace, I first **highlight the paragraph**. By doing so, I guarantee that the Find and Replace function will go **NO FURTHER** than the highlighted material thus giving me more control over the document. Of course, if I just run a Find and Replace and say "**Replace All**" I may not see any error that was made repeatedly especially if I am dealing with a rather large document. Doing it in piecemeal does help to avoid bad mistakes with large files.

A. **Control H**. brings up your **Find and Replace** Dialog Box

B. In the **Find What** area type in a **Closed Parenthesis** and a regular space

C. In the **Replace with** area put in a Closed Parenthesis and Click the "**More**" Button followed by the "**Special**" Button and select **Non-Breaking Space**.

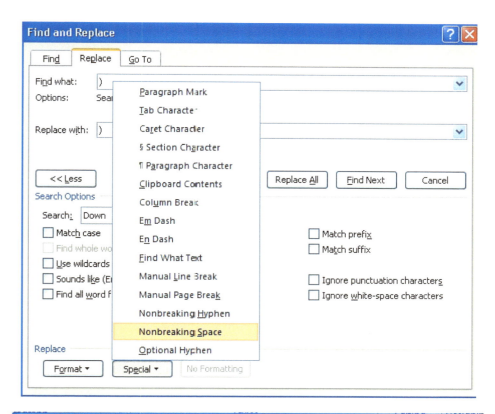

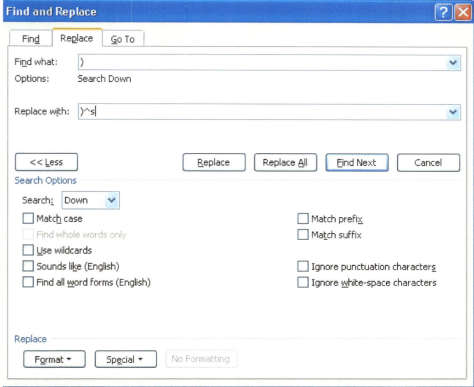

D.   Select **Replace All** and all of the areas in need of hard space protection should now be done. You may wish to highlight a paragraph at a time or a number of paragraphs at a time and run the replace. **Having the paragraph(s) highlighted will force the "Replace" function to stop**, tell you how many instances have been replaced and thus giving you the ability to go forward **and/or stop** the global replace as needed.

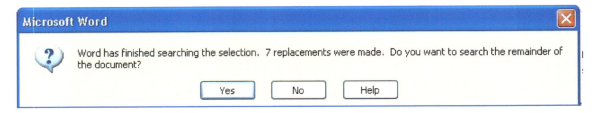

E.   For those situations whereby you need to protect a hyphenated area such as "**above-mentioned**", you will use **Control + Shift + Hyphen** which will then guarantee that the hyphenated words will never separate.

CHAPTER 14.
MAKING USE OF THE CLIPBOARD
WHEN APPLYING STYLES

Scenario: Styles are being applied to a large file. You have **Heading Styles** for the **Multilevel Outline**, **Body Text Styles** for the **non-numbered paragraphs** and a **Style Separator** scenario whereby the text to the right of the style separator uses a **Body Text Type Style** to **disassociate** the remaining Body Text from the **Heading 2** that sits **before** the Style Separator. Below, look at "**Heading 2**" in the picture for an example of such a paragraph.

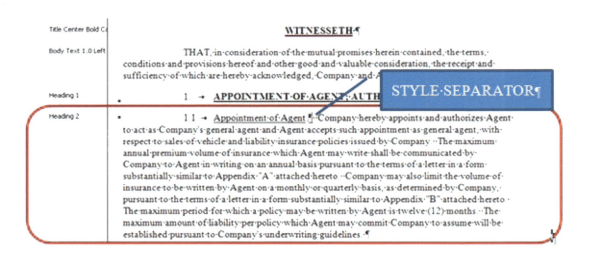

When putting together an involved document, you don't want to have to go up and down the right side style pallet looking for each needed style. That eats up a lot of time and results in **a lot of unnecessary movement**.

Instead, we can use a combination of things in order to smooth out the process of applying styles.

Back to the Style Separator Example:

1.   You have the **right side Palette Open** where you are starring at Heading 2.

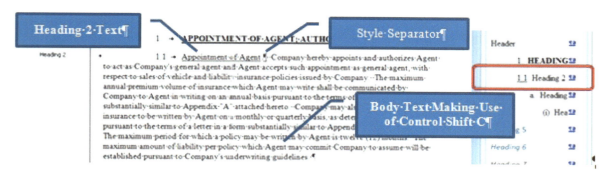

2.   After we bring in the **first instance** of the **Body Text Style** that is applied **after** the **Style Separator**, we can place the formatting of that style we will be using again and again on your "**Clipboard**" by the use of **Control Shift C**. This body text style that disassociates the text from Heading 2 will now be copied and available all day as needed on your Clipboard until of course, you establish a new instance of Control Shift C.

The Sequence:

1.   Apply the **Heading 2** style to the text that **shares the paragraph**. Heading 2 and its attributes connected to it come in.

2.   Secondly, apply the **Style Separator.** 1) Place your cursor after the period at the end of the Heading 2 text. **In the example above, the end of the Heading 2 text is the word "Agent".** 2) You make a **return** and then immediately **bring your cursor right back up** to where you just made your return, 3) **Use Control Alt Enter to insert the Style Separator** and your cursor will now **be sitting to the right** of the Style Separator.

3.   Use **Control Shift V** to paste the formatting of the Body Text style you placed on the clipboard that **disassociates the body text from the Heading 2 text**.

4.   This method will help to cut down on much of the movement associated with applying styles. The use of the **Control Shift V** is more efficient than using the Paint Brush because you have to go up to Home then Paint each and every time to make use of the Paint Brush opposed to just using Control Shift V. **FYI**: **Control Shift C** and **Control Shift V** is the **control key combination** equal to the use of the **Paint Brush**.

7.   In sum, placing **your most used style of the particular document** you are working on onto your clipboard will make the process of applying styles a lot easier for that particular editing session.

CHAPTER 15.
CHANGING THE FONT FOR THE ENTIRE DOCUMENT

Okay, the experienced secretaries and operators will say "tell me something new". I have the experienced beginners through advanced operators and secretaries so I see on a regular basis simple things that cause a problem to those who may have never come across the request to change the font throughout the entire document. Where and when does this occur?

1.   On many hands on WP tests, either in a law firm or within an agency, I have seen within the instructions to change the text of the document from one font to another. So the test taker sits down and brings up the test which for example is in Ariel 12 as part of the test instructions. This same type of request can come from an attorney that has a client that wants a particular font used or a court that wants documents submitted in a particular font.

2.   Students are a great source of how the mind works before they find out the proper way to quickly do this procedure. Some of the ways they choose to go about this request are the following:

A.   They grab the entire document by using Control A and simply change the font. This is "Direct" type formatting and is not the way to go.

B.   Others very carefully take stock of all the styles they are presently using in the document and then they modify each individual style over to the requested new font. This is better, but each new style you either create or activate from the right side palette you will have to remember to switch the font over to the new font otherwise, you will have a mixture of fonts throughout the entire document.

C.   Finally, knowing that every paragraph style if properly created, is based on "Normal", *WE SIMPLY MODIFY NORMAL* which results in the immediate switch over of the current font to the new requested font and for any new styles that you may create in that document will automatically now revert to the new font.

D.   This does come up more than you may think so now you know how to quickly take care of this request.

CHAPTER 16. QUOTES
SMART VS. STRAIGHT

This also made this book for the simple reason that the amount of time you spend on a document, will make you or break you in a WP Law Firm Center. If you are dealing with a large file and trying to pick through hundreds of quotes in order to change them from straight to smart or vice versa, this can be very time consuming. You need to be able to do a **Global Replace** that will take care of this for you from top to bottom. By having the ability to do so, you can then relax and concentrate of the real task of doing your edits or formatting the document.

Every law firm is different. Some firms may officially use Straight Quotes "**Straight**" and some may use **"Smart"** The Straight Quotes are Straight up and down and the Smart Quotes or sometimes referred to as **Curly Quotes** are curved on each side of the quote.

So you may be asking **what is the big deal**? Well due to the fact that a lot of documents go from 10 pages to 110 pages you may be in a situation where throughout the document you have **a combination** of both **straight quotes** and **smart quotes** mixed in. If the attorney spots this, they will often make a note on the document to make **all quotes either straight or smart according to their preference. Firm style is important, but attorney preference always wins out**!

If you **do not** know how to go about this, you will be in a position where you are going through let's say a 75 page document and changing the quotes to the attorney preference one by one. What if there are **500 of them to fix**? Also, in this scenario **you are bound to miss some of them** so the document **will continue to have a mixture** of Straight and Smart and **you will only get on the nerves of the attorney** who will voice his/her displeasure to the Coordinator. **Lucky you!** So below, I am going to start out by showing you how to prep a document to globally change all quotes in the document over to Smart Quotes.

Globally Change All Quotes In The Document Over To Smart Quotes

1.   Go to **File Options**, **Proofing**.

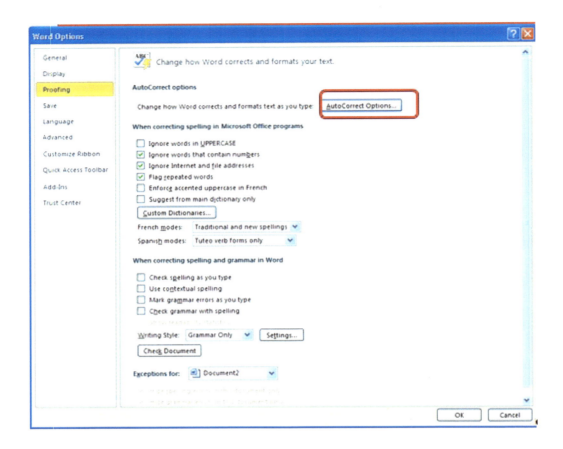

2.   Click on "**Autocorrect Options**".

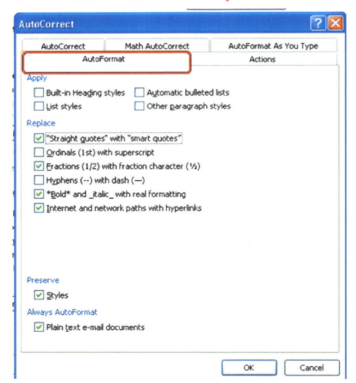

3.	Under **Auto Format, place** a check ☑ next to **Straight Quotes with Smart Quotes**.

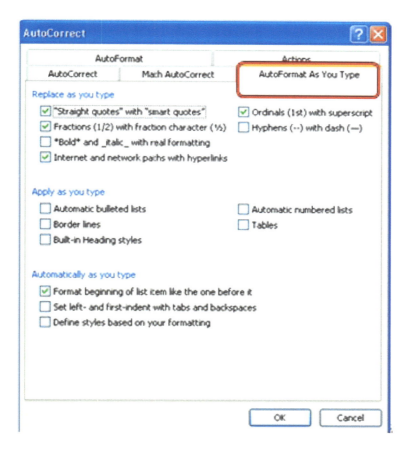

4.	Under **Auto Format as you Type**, place a check ☑ next to Straight Quotes with Smart Quotes. Now that the system knows that we **only want Smart Quotes**, we will now perform a global replace in order to **uniformly** change all quotes over to Smart Quotes throughout the **entire** document.

5.	Use **Control + H**. and the Find and Replace Dialog box will appear. In the **Find What** area type in a **quote (yes just a plain quote)**. In the **Replace With** area type in a quote. Because we had **earlier changed the instruction under Auto Format and Auto Format as You Type over to the Smart** style quotes, the system will **turn every quote it finds,** into a **smart quote** as it goes through the Global Replace. Once the global replace has finished, your document will have all Smart Quotes. **That is guaranteed**. Below is how the Find and Replace Dialog box should look right before you run the Global Replace.

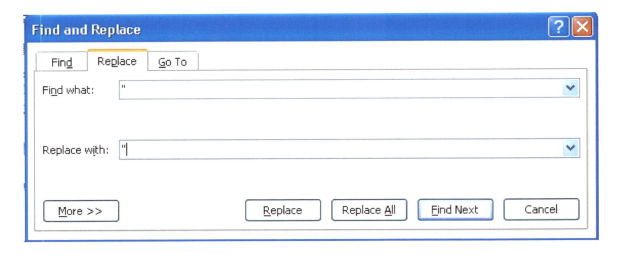

6.   If you were to do them one by one, you are most likely going to miss a few. Below is a sample from a document showing that all of the Quotes have been converted to Smart quotes.

"Drawdown Date" means the date on which an Advance is made pursuant to Clause 2 (*The Facility*):

"Drawdown Conditions" shall have the meaning defined in Clause 4:

"Drawdown Request" means a notice substantially in the form attached at Schedule 2:

"Event of Default" means any event or circumstance specified as such in Clause 16 (*Events of Default*):

"Existing Borrower Loans" means the various existing loans to the Borrower, brief particulars of which are set out in Schedule 4:

"Facility" means the loan facility made available under this Agreement as described and defined in Clause 2.1:

"Finance Document" means this Agreement the Security Documents and any other document designated a "Finance Document" by the Lender and the Borrower, and for the avoidance of doubt shall include any Step-Up Loan Agreement entered into by the Borrower and the Lender, or its Affiliate, pursuant to Clause 9.1 of the JACK VANCE Agreement (and the term "Finance Documents" means more than one of them):

Making The Document Uniform For Straight Quotes.

1.   Go back to File, Options, Proofing, Autocorrect Options.

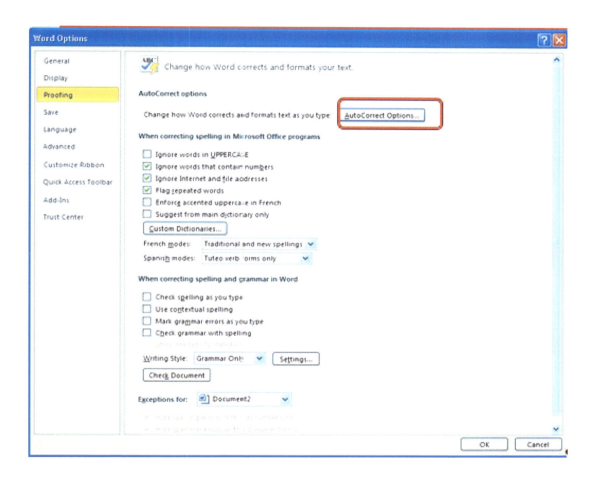

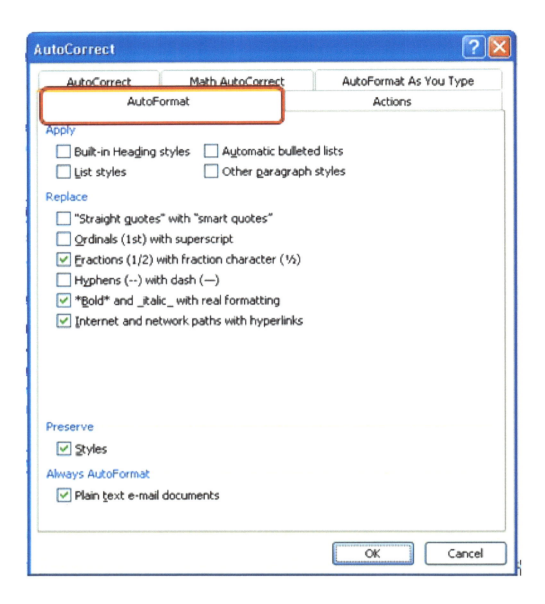

2.   Under **Auto Format** **remove the check** next to **Straight Quotes with Smart Quotes**.

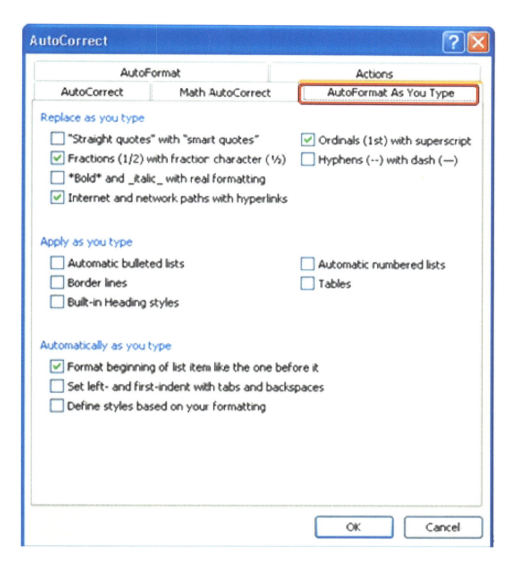

3.   Under **Auto Format As You Type**, **remove the check** next to **Straight Quotes with Smart Quotes**. Now that the system knows, we only want **Straight Quotes**, we will now perform a global replace in order to **Uniformly change all quotes over to Straight Quotes** throughout the entire document.

4.   **Use Control + H**. and in the **Find What** area type in a quote (just a plain ole quote). In the Replace With area, type in a quote. Because we had earlier changed the instruction under **Auto Format** and **Auto Format as You Type** over to Straight Quotes the system knows what to do as it comes across each quote in the Global Replace. Once the global replace has finished, your document will have all **Straight Quotes**. That is guaranteed. If you do them one by one (manually) you are most likely going to miss a few. Also, if you do them one by one you place a lot of stress on yourself, because most likely someone is waiting on the document. This routine will serve you well and you will have plenty of opportunity to use it throughout your shifts.

CHAPTER 17. BONUS
RUNNING A TABLE OF CONTENTS IN TWO COLUMNS

This subject will come up from time to time at work and it will come up from time to time on a hands-on word processing test. Running your TOC in a two column format is rather simple but it does have a routine that needs to be followed so let's go over it. Of course, we are using the "Heading" styles to represent each separate Multilevel Outline Level of our document.

Most of the time, this is being done because the document is rather large and instead of having 5 pages of Table of Contents entries they want to significantly shorten it. Because of this, we would be wise to use the Table of Contents method where the **TOC has it own dedicated section** and the Table of Contents and Page titles are placed in the **Header** of that Section.

So let's get this going.

1.   In your document, after your cover page, we have a section break. Now your TOC comes in. After your TOC make a section break. Your Table of Contents Heading will be placed in the **First Page Header of Section 2**. When it spills over one page the **Second Header of Section 2** (because of the different first page option) will be set-up to say **Table of Contents (continued)** as shown in the pictures below.

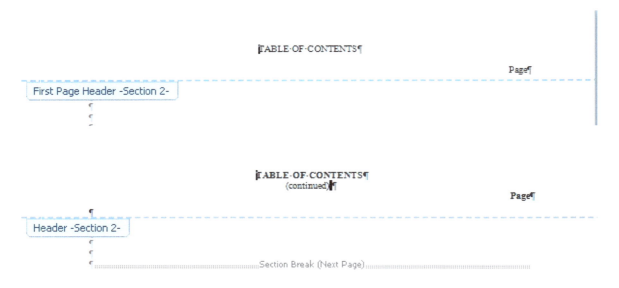

2.   Now that your heading is in place, we can focus on the running of the Table of Contents. **Run the Table of Contents as usual**. The picture at the top of the next page assumes you just ran your Table of Contents.

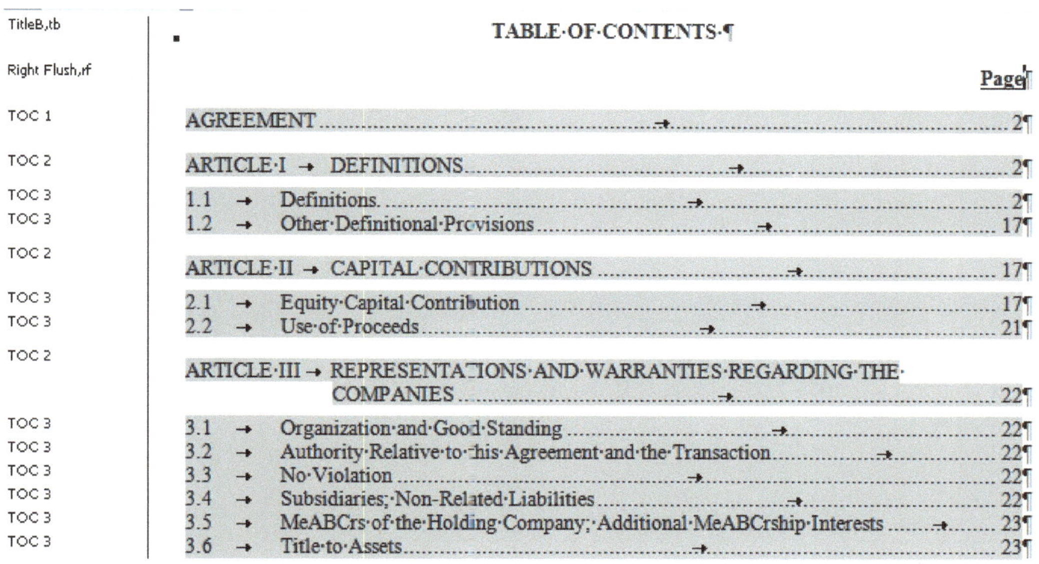

TitleB,tb

Right Flush,rf

TABLE·OF·CONTENTS·¶

Page¶

TOC 1 AGREEMENT ....→..............2¶

TOC 2 ARTICLE·I → DEFINITIONS...............................→..............2¶
TOC 3 1.1 → Definitions.....................................→............2¶
TOC 3 1.2 → Other·Definitional·Provisions ....→.............17¶

TOC 2 ARTICLE·II → CAPITAL·CONTRIBUTIONS ....→.............17¶

TOC 3 2.1 → Equity·Capital·Contribution ....→.............17¶
TOC 3 2.2 → Use·of·Proceeds ....→.............21¶

TOC 2 ARTICLE·III → REPRESENTATIONS·AND·WARRANTIES·REGARDING·THE·
              COMPANIES ....→.............22¶

TOC 3 3.1 → Organization·and·Good·Standing ....→.............22¶
TOC 3 3.2 → Authority·Relative·to·his·Agreement·and·the·Transaction....→.........22¶
TOC 3 3.3 → No·Violation ....→.............22¶
TOC 3 3.4 → Subsidiaries;·Non-Related·Liabilities ......→.............22¶
TOC 3 3.5 → MeABCrs·of·the·Holding·Company;·Additional·MeABCrship·Interests ....→........23¶
TOC 3 3.6 → Title·to·Assets ....→.............23¶

3.   Two things to do in TOC 1, TOC 2 and TOC 3. My sample happens to have 3 sections that are utilized in the TOC but **most** will have two. You can enter TOC 1 TOC 2 and TOC 3, by **double clicking** on the style name in the left side panel as long as you are in **Draft** view

4.   In each of the above-mentioned TOC sections, I want you to modify them and change the **font** down to **8pt**. Then go Tabs, and under Tabs **clear out** the current Tab that controls the page numbers and replace it with a **Tab at 3.0** on the ruler. Make sure the Tab is set for "**Right Tab**" and apply a **dotted line leader** which is number **2.** as shown in the picture below.

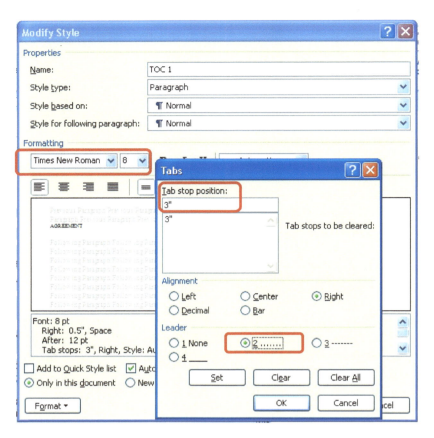

5.   Keep in mind that **after each heading**, there is a tab before the **words of that heading** so that has to be adjusted as well. So let me show you how that would look. In our example, if you look back a page, the two tab situation, did not come into play **until TOC 2** but many times there will be a heading number followed by text on **TOC 1** as well.

6.   The **0.7** example, should have **a left tab alignment** while the **3.0** which represents and controls **the page numbers on the right**, should **have right alignment and a dotted line leader attached to it**.

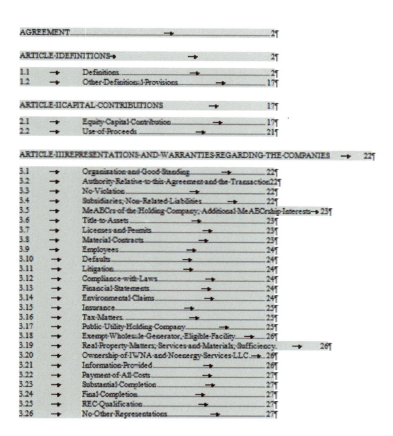

7.   Okay, we have **not** put on the Columns feature yet. Above, your TOC should look something like this sample at this point. Do not worry too much about those areas that jut out because when we create the two column look, they will correct themselves.

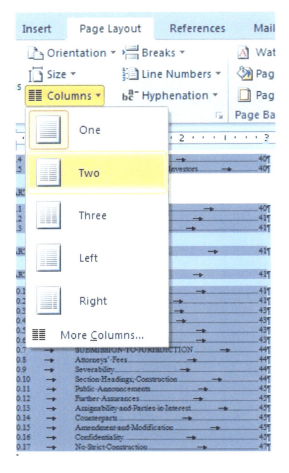

8.	As shown above, **highlight the entire TOC** then go to Page Layout, Columns and select Two.

9.	When you select Two, your TOC will divide into two columns and you will still have the word "Page" in your header but it will only **be on one side** and **not** the left side as shown below.

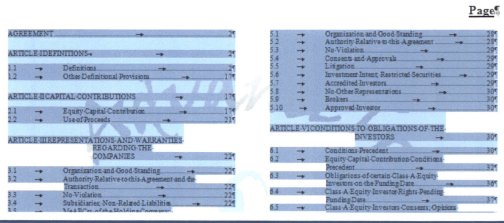

11.   There are **two ways to go** as to the word "**Page**". We can either 1) delete the word Page altogether or we can create **a two column one row table** in the **header** and place the word "**Page**" over each set of page numbers in the TOC. Let us assume that we have decided to place the word "**Page**" over **both sets of numbers** for the TOC pages.

12.   In your header, make a **two column 1 row table**. In each cell of the table, do **Control R** and type in "**Page**". That will throw the word "**Page**" to the **extreme right** of each cell. Now, manipulate the cells so that the word **Page** from each cell sits nicely over the page numbers. Take a look at the picture below, and note that I took off the borders of the table that contains the word **Page** in each cell.

TABLE·OF·CONTENTS¶

		Page					Page
AGREEMENT	→	2¶	5.1	→	Organization·and·Good·Standing	→	28¶
			5.2	→	Authority·Relative·to·this·Agreement	→	28¶
ARTICLE·I·DEFINITIONS→	→	2¶	5.3	→	No·Violation		29¶
			5.4	→	Consents·and·Approvals	→	29¶
1.1 → Definitions	→	2¶	5.5	→	Litigation		29¶
1.2 → Other·Definitional·Provisions	→	17¶	5.6	→	Investment·Intent;·Restricted·Securities	→	29¶
			5.7	→	Accredited·Investors	→	29¶
ARTICLE·II·CAPITAL·CONTRIBUTIONS	→	17¶	5.8	→	No·Other·Representations	→	30¶
			5.9	→	Brokers		30¶
2.1 → Equity·Capital·Contribution	→	17¶	5.10	→	Approved·Investor		30¶
2.2 → Use·of·Proceeds	→	21¶					

13.   Finally, when dealing with columns, you should know that when you are in **Draft view**, the columns will appear as **one long column**. If for any reason, you need to break the column up **at a different location** than it is currently breaking, then while in **Draft view**, you do **Control Shift Enter** and that is a **column break** which is what you use to segment a column as needed. Most probably you will not have to use this.

14.   *An alternative method* is to run the TOC, Highlight the TOC and under Page Layout or "Layout" in 2016, choose 2 columns and switch to Draft View.

15.   In Draft View, look very closely at the right side of the ruler and you will see a very light right tab in the ruler. Tug that tab all the way over to the left side approximately at 3.0 or so on the ruler. Yes, you can tug the right tab across the boundaries of the two separate columns.

16.   Switch back to the Print Layout view to see the results.

CHAPTER 18. CONCLUSION

So, we are at the end of the Strategy Session Volume 2. We give class every week in terms of MS Word Legal 2007-19. Classes are small and are done both in person as well as over the phone and we can also come to your office. Go to www.advanceto.com and check us out. This training from day 1 will place you in the atmosphere, strategy, judgment and thinking process that those of us in the legal industry use every day. This is a small club that operates in the way that we do. When you know this style of MS Word, you place yourself in the top 5% of those doing MS Word for a living.

To get a very good idea at the type of material we cover, I urge you to join us on LinkedIn at *AdvanceTo Legal and Corporate Word Processing Training Forum*. Hundreds of top-tier level how to articles since 2010.

When you are finished with our training, you will be at expert level. We work directly with you until you go out to the job agencies. We also do test prep so you truly know what to expect and we have a number of agencies we deal with that have major legal firms as clients. We will target you to them if you so choose.

You can find me personally at Facebook.com/legaltestready.

Take what you learned from this book and incorporate it into your everyday work.

I wish you the best.

Louis

louisellman@gmail.com

louis@advanceto.com

888-422-0692 Ext. 2